one-bowl
MEALS

one-bowl
MEALS

Tonia George

photography by William Reavell

RYLAND
PETERS
& SMALL
LONDON NEW YORK

First published in the
United States in 2007
by Ryland Peters & Small, Inc.
519 Broadway, 5th Floor
New York, NY 10012

www.rylandpeters.com

10 9 8 7 6 5 4 3 2 1

ISBN-13: 978 1 84597 471 8
ISBN-10: 1 84597 471 9

Library of Congress Cataloging-in-
Publication Data

George, Tonia.
  One-bowl meals / Tonia George ;
photography by William Reavell.
    p. cm.
  Includes index.
  ISBN 978-1-84597-471-8
  1. One-dish meals. I. Title.
  TX840.O53G45 2007
  641.8'2--dc22
                    2007011045

Designers Toni Kay and Carl Hodson
Editor Céline Hughes
Production Patricia Harrington
Publishing Director Alison Starling

Food Stylist Tonia George
Prop Stylist Liz Hippisley
Americanizer Susan Stuck
Indexer Hilary Bird

Author's acknowledgments
Thanks to my father for his wonderful
cooking genes, my mother, and indeed
my mother-in-law for thinking every
cookbook I produce is the best in the
world, and both of them for their good
taste. Well done to Bill Reavell for his
wonderful photographs; to Seiko who
helped me cook all the food for the
shoot, and Jo who helped me taste
and test each recipe. Thank you to
RPS, Alison, and Céline for giving me
the project and producing such lovely
little books that all set a really high
standard. And finally, thanks to my
husband for reasons that are far too
slushy to pen here!

Notes
• All spoon measurements are level,
unless otherwise specified.
• All eggs are medium, unless
otherwise specified. Uncooked or
partially cooked eggs should not be
served to the very young, the very old,
those with compromised immune
systems, or to pregnant women.

Contents

Food for the soul

A handsomely decorated dining table laden with dishes might be the perfect place to gather with friends and family on the weekend, but the mood of a weekday is different. I love the informality of a bowl of slippery noodles and a glass of cold beer at the kitchen table. Or, when the rain is pattering on the window panes, I confess that I'll happily eat off my lap, curled up on the sofa in front of a good movie. Sometimes all I crave is a lusty bowl of soup and some crusty bread to dredge across it when I'm done.

Cooking supper is a meditative time for me and it rewards me for my day's efforts. Some of my best meals have come about from those creative moments when, after a long day, I have searched in my cupboards and fridge and found inspiration. Lots of meals in this book started life this way, and became comforting, tasty, satisfying bowl food with a little help from some easy-to-buy ingredients.

Strictly speaking of course, desserts are not vital, but sometimes a meal just isn't complete without a sweet treat to round it off.

Grab a bowl of comfort food, relax, and enjoy.

Winter-spiced salad
with pears, honeyed pecans, and ricotta

1 star anise

1 cinnamon stick

2 pears, unpeeled, quartered, and cored

5 oz mixed salad greens, such as arugula, shredded radicchio, or baby Swiss chard

4 oz fresh ricotta, preferably buffalo milk ricotta

Honeyed pecans

¼ cup pecans

¼ teaspoon dried red pepper flakes

¼ teaspoon fennel seeds

3 tablespoons honey

Dressing

¼ cup safflower oil

1 tablespoon walnut oil

freshly squeezed juice of 1 lemon

1 large red chile, partly seeded and chopped

Serves 4

You need to be careful when buying fresh ricotta because it can sometimes be very soggy, especially when sold in tubs. I find the organic varieties or buffalo ricotta crumbly rather than creamy, which is what you're after here. Buffalo mozzarella also works well, as does a soft, fresh goat cheese. Leave some seeds in the chile to give a little kick, awaken all the other flavors, and contrast with the sweet nuts.

Fill a saucepan with water and add the star anise and cinnamon stick. Bring to a boil and add the pears. Poach for 12 minutes, or until tender.

Put the pecans, a large pinch of salt, the red pepper flakes, and the fennel seeds in a skillet and toast until golden and aromatic. Pour in the honey, turn the heat right up, and let bubble away for a few minutes. Tip onto parchment paper and let cool.

Meanwhile, to make the dressing, beat together the safflower and walnut oils, the lemon juice, and chile.

Transfer the mixed greens to bowls, scatter over the pears, and crumble over the ricotta. Drizzle with the dressing. Roughly break up the nuts with your fingers and scatter them over the top.

Soups and Salads

There's no dressing as such for this dish because the roasting chorizo produces a wonderful paprika-scented oil. The juices should be really hot so they wilt the spinach slightly. With the sweet potato, meaty chorizo, and salty cheese, this is much more than a salad.

Sweet potato salad
with black olives, chorizo, and feta cheese

1 ¼ lb sweet potatoes, peeled and cut into wedges

2 tablespoons extra virgin olive oil

2 fresh rosemary sprigs, broken up into smaller sprigs

½ teaspoon dried red pepper flakes

8 oz chorizo, sliced

3 tablespoons sherry vinegar

6½ oz baby spinach, washed and dried

½ cup black olives, pitted and chopped

6 oz feta cheese

Serves 4

Preheat the oven to 375°F.

Place the sweet potatoes in a roasting pan, drizzle with the olive oil, and sprinkle with the rosemary and red pepper flakes. Roast for 10 minutes until beginning to soften.

Add the chorizo and roast for a further 15 minutes until the chorizo is crispy and the sweet potato is softening and blackening nicely.

At the end of the cooking time, drizzle over the vinegar and return to the oven for a further 5 minutes.

Transfer the spinach to bowls and top with the sweet potato, chorizo, olives, and feta. Drizzle the juices from the roasting pan over the salad and stir well before serving.

Puy lentils, grown in France, are very fashionable but they are also great at thickening soups without turning sludgy. They give this soup a pert little bite which is offset by the soft, buttery vegetables and enriched by the heady tang of the dried oregano.

Chunky Puy lentil and vegetable soup

3 tablespoons butter

2 carrots, finely chopped

2 leeks, white part only, thinly sliced

1 large onion, finely chopped

3 garlic cloves, sliced

½ teaspoon dried red pepper flakes

2 teaspoons dried oregano

a 14-oz can chopped plum tomatoes

1 cup small green lentils, preferably French Puy lentils

1 quart vegetable stock

sea salt and freshly ground black pepper

freshly grated pecorino or Parmesan cheese, to serve

crusty bread, toasted and buttered, to serve

Serves 4-6

Melt the butter in a heavy-based saucepan. Add the carrots, leeks, onion, and garlic and a large pinch of salt. Stir until everything is coated in butter and cook over medium heat, with the lid on, for 15 minutes, stirring occasionally.

Once the vegetables have softened, add the red pepper flakes, oregano, tomatoes, lentils, and stock. Cover again and let simmer for 30 minutes, or until the lentils are cooked. Season with salt and freshly ground pepper to taste.

Transfer to bowls and serve with buttered toast and grated pecorino or Parmesan cheese on the side.

Minty pea risotto soup

2 tablespoons butter

1 onion, finely chopped

5 oz pancetta, cubed

14 oz frozen peas, defrosted, or fresh if available

2 tablespoons extra virgin olive oil, plus extra for drizzling

¾ cup risotto rice

1½ quarts chicken or vegetable stock, plus extra if necessary

2 tablespoons fresh mint, shredded

sea salt and freshly ground black pepper

grated Parmesan cheese, to serve

Serves 4–6

This is loosely based on the Venetian dish *risi e bisi*, which uses new season peas. It's a cross between a soup and a risotto and should be soupy in consistency. If it's the season for English peas, do use them, but I find myself cooking this when there's nothing else at hand—one always has a bag of peas in the freezer and the other ingredients are easy to buy.

Melt the butter in a medium saucepan, then add the onion and pancetta. Cook over low/medium heat, with the lid on, for 8 minutes, or until the onion is softened and translucent. Stir occasionally.

Meanwhile, put half the peas in a food processor with the olive oil and blend until puréed.

Add the rice to the softening onion and stir until well coated in butter. Pour in the stock and add the puréed peas. Simmer, uncovered, for 15 minutes.

Add the remaining peas, season well, and cook for a further 8–10 minutes, or until the rice is tender. Stir in the mint and add a little more stock if you think it needs to be soupier.

Transfer to bowls, drizzle with olive oil, and scatter with freshly ground black pepper. Serve with grated Parmesan cheese.

Chickpea, tomato, and chorizo soup

6 oz chorizo, roughly chopped

1 red onion, chopped

2 garlic cloves, peeled
and crushed

a 14-oz can chopped
plum tomatoes

2 fresh thyme sprigs

a 14-oz can chickpeas,
drained and rinsed

1 quart vegetable stock

sea salt and freshly ground
black pepper

Serves 4

I have found that most dishes containing chorizo taste pretty good. This soup is no exception and needs no embellishments, making it refreshingly simple to prepare. Make sure you buy the correct chorizo—you want the short, fat, little cured sausages. They are ready to eat but are so much better fried and crispy.

Put the chorizo in a large saucepan or casserole dish over medium heat and cook until it starts to release its oil. Continue to cook, stirring, for 4–5 minutes until it is brown and crisp.

Add the red onion and garlic and turn the heat right down to allow them to soften in the chorizo's paprika-infused oil. After 6–7 minutes the onion and garlic should be translucent and glossy. Add the tomatoes and thyme and turn the heat back up. Cook for 5 minutes to intensify the flavor, then add the chickpeas and stock. Return to a boil, cover, and simmer for 15 minutes.

Remove the thyme. Season well with salt and freshly ground black pepper and simmer for a further 10 minutes to allow all the flavors to get to know one another.

Transfer to bowls and serve.

Tagliatelle with peas
and goat cheese pesto

8 oz fresh or frozen peas (thawed)

14 oz tagliatelle

freshly grated Parmesan cheese, to serve

sea salt and freshly ground black pepper

Pesto

1 small garlic clove

2 large green chiles, deseeded

2 handfuls of fresh basil leaves, plus extra to serve

3 tablespoons pine nuts

⅛ cup extra virgin olive oil

3½ oz goat cheese

Serves 4

Crumbly goat cheese works surprisingly well in pesto, adding a slightly creamy edge to it. Roughly crumble it in so you get pockets of the molten cheese tucked in among your tangle of tagliatelle.

To make the pesto, put the garlic, chiles, basil, and a large pinch of salt in a food processor and process until roughly chopped. Alternatively, crush everything with a pestle and mortar.

Put the pine nuts in a dry skillet and toast over low heat for a few minutes, shaking the skillet, until they are golden all over. Add the pine nuts to the mixture in the food processor (or the mortar) and process again until coarsely chopped. Add half the olive oil and process again. Add the remaining oil, crumble in the goat cheese, and stir. Taste and season.

Bring a large saucepan of salted water and a small pan of unsalted water to a boil. Add the peas to the smaller pan and simmer for 4–5 minutes if fresh or 3 minutes if frozen. Once the water in the large pot comes to a rolling boil, add the tagliatelle and cook according to the manufacturer's instructions until it is al dente. Drain and tip back into the pan.

Add 2–3 good dollops of pesto and the peas to the tagliatelle and toss through the hot strands, then add the remaining pesto making sure all the pasta is thoroughly coated. Transfer to bowls and sprinkle with basil and freshly grated Parmesan.

Pad thai

6½ oz flat medium rice noodles

2 tablespoons tamarind paste

3 tablespoons Thai fish sauce

3 tablespoons palm sugar or
natural cane sugar

2 tablespoons safflower oil

3 garlic cloves, peeled
and crushed

8 oz uncooked tiger shrimp,
shelled and deveined but
tails intact

⅓ cup unsalted peanuts,
chopped

½ teaspoon dried red
pepper flakes

2 eggs, beaten

1 cup beansprouts

4 scallions, shredded

lime wedges, to serve

Serves 2

Thai food always presents the palate with a kaleidoscope of flavors and the knack is getting the balance just right. Pad thai needs to be really sweet and soothing, but the tamarind and lime give it a fruity tang of sourness and the fish sauce provides a characteristic salty depth.

Put the noodles in a large bowl and cover with boiling water. Let soften for 5 minutes. (Check the manufacturer's instructions because some cooking methods vary.) Combine the tamarind paste, fish sauce, and sugar and set aside.

Heat the oil in a wok or large skillet over medium heat and add the garlic. Stir-fry until the garlic is beginning to color, then add the shrimp, peanuts, and red pepper flakes. Stir-fry for another 2–3 minutes, or until the shrimp turn pink and the nuts are golden.

Drain the noodles well and add to the wok along with the tamarind mixture. Toss until everything is evenly coated and push to one side of the wok. Pour the egg into a corner of the wok and cook until it is scrambled and dry, then stir into the noodle mixture. Add the beansprouts and scallions, give it one final toss, and transfer to bowls. Serve with a few lime wedges on the side.

There's something pure about *linguine alle vongole*, which is redolent of the seaside and its salty air. The cherry tomatoes and tarragon here are my own touch and they freshen up the whole thing. If you can't get fresh clams, used canned ones or mussels instead.

Linguine alle vongole
with tarragon and cherry tomatoes

1½ lb littleneck clams, cleaned and scrubbed

⅔ cup dry white wine or vermouth

12 oz linguine

⅓ cup extra virgin olive oil

2 garlic cloves, peeled and thinly sliced

¼ teaspoon dried red pepper flakes

8 oz small cherry tomatoes, halved

3 fresh tarragon sprigs, finely chopped

freshly ground black pepper

Serves 4

Put a large saucepan of salted water on to boil for the linguine.

Discard any clams that do not shut when tapped sharply against the worktop. Pour the white wine into another large saucepan and bring to a boil over high heat, then add the clams. Cover tightly with a lid, wait a couple of minutes, then stir so the unopened clams fall to the bottom. Replace the lid and cook for a further 2 minutes. By this time all the clams should be open; discard any that remain closed. Transfer the remainder to a bowl with all the juices and reserve the saucepan for later.

When the salted water in the large saucepan is boiling, add the linguine and cook according to the manufacturer's instructions until al dente. In the clam pan, heat half the olive oil, then add the garlic, red pepper flakes, and cherry tomatoes. Cook over medium heat for a few minutes until the tomatoes burst and soften. Spoon in the cooked clams and strain in ¾ cup of the cooking liquid. Cook over high heat until the liquid boils. Drain the cooked linguine and add to the pan with the clams. Toss in the tarragon, the remaining olive oil, and lots of freshly ground black pepper. Serve immediately.

Pappardelle with breaded chicken
and garlic-parsley butter

3 skinless chicken breasts

1 egg, beaten

**¾ cup fresh white
bread crumbs**

¼ cup flour

**3–4 tablespoons extra virgin
olive oil**

10 oz pappardelle

5 tablespoons butter

**2 garlic cloves, peeled
and crushed**

**a small handful of fresh
flatleaf parsley, chopped**

**1 oz Parmesan cheese
shavings**

**sea salt and freshly ground
black pepper**

a large freezer bag

Serves 4

Here are all the flavors and crunch of chicken Kiev, which I find inexplicably nostalgic. Of course, making your own is not only much tastier, but with thick strands of pappardelle to soak up the buttery juices, it's good bowl food, too. Turkey escalopes or cod fillets work just as well.

Put a large saucepan of salted water on to boil for the pappardelle.

Prepare one bowl with the beaten egg and another with the bread crumbs. Put one chicken breast in the freezer bag and bash with a rolling pin until flattened out. Spoon some of the flour into the bag, season well, and shake until the chicken is coated. Dip the chicken in the egg, then in the bread crumbs and set aside. Repeat the entire process with the remaining chicken breasts.

Heat the oil in a large skillet over medium heat and add the chicken in a single layer. Cook for 2–3 minutes, then turn over and cook the other side for the same amount of time, or until both sides are golden. When the salted water in the large pan is boiling, add the pappardelle and cook according to the manufacturer's instructions until al dente. Lift the chicken onto a cutting board. Add the butter to the skillet along with the garlic and parsley and let cook over low heat until the garlic and butter are about to color. Season generously. Cut the chicken into strips and return to the skillet.

Drain the pappardelle (reserving a cup of the water), slide it all back into the pan you cooked it in, and tip in the chicken with all its juices. Give it a good stir, add the reserved cup of water to keep the pasta moist, and transfer to bowls. Sprinkle with Parmesan shavings.

In Italy, pork is often braised with milk, as it tenderizes the meat and the juices mingle with the milk to provide a sweet, meaty sauce. Rosemary is lovely and robust with pork but you could use chopped sage—just add it earlier when you brown the pork so it frazzles a little.

Rigatoni with pork and lemon ragu

2 tablespoons olive oil

14 oz ground pork

1 onion, finely chopped

2 garlic cloves, peeled and thinly sliced

4 anchovy fillets in oil, drained

2 tablespoons rosemary leaves

finely grated peel and juice of 1 unwaxed lemon

12 oz rigatoni

2 cups whole milk

⅔ cup green olives, pitted and chopped

⅓ cup heavy cream

a good grating of fresh nutmeg

¼ cup Parmesan cheese shavings, plus extra to serve

sea salt and freshly ground black pepper

Serves 4

Put a large saucepan of salted water on to boil for the rigatoni.

Meanwhile, heat the olive oil in a large skillet over high heat and add the pork. Leave it for a few minutes until it browns, then turn it over and allow the other side to brown too. Add the onion, garlic, anchovies, rosemary, and lemon peel and stir to combine with the pork. Reduce the heat, cover, and let the onion soften for 10 minutes, stirring occasionally so the ingredients don't stick to the bottom of the skillet.

When the salted water in the large pan is boiling, add the rigatoni and cook according to the manufacturer's instructions until al dente.

When the onion is translucent, add the milk, lemon juice, and olives, and bring to a boil, uncovered, scraping the base of the skillet to loosen any sticky, flavorful bits and incorporating them into the sauce. Simmer for about 15–20 minutes, or until about two-thirds of the liquid has evaporated and the pork is soft. Stir in the cream, then season with salt, pepper, and nutmeg.

Drain the rigatoni, put it back into its pan, and spoon in the pork ragu. Add the Parmesan shavings, stir well, and transfer to bowls. Sprinkle the extra Parmesan shavings on top.

Beef polpetti
with tomato sauce and spaghetti

10–12 oz spaghetti

sea salt and freshly ground black pepper

Tomato sauce

¼ cup extra virgin olive oil

3 cloves garlic, peeled and thinly sliced

1 large onion, cut into wedges

two 14-oz cans chopped plum tomatoes

a handful of fresh basil, plus extra to serve

Meatballs

8 oz ground beef

1 cup fresh white bread crumbs

2 eggs

2 tablespoons freshly grated Parmesan cheese, plus extra to serve

¼ cup chopped fresh parsley

3 tablespoons extra virgin olive oil

Serves 4

I learned how to make *polpetti*—Italian meatballs—from a friend's granny in Rome. I watched as she poured in the most enormous amount of bread crumbs—I assumed she was being thrifty but then I tried them and realized that the bread lightens them and absorbs much more of the sauce and flavorful oil released by the meat. A simple tomato sauce is all that's needed, accompanied by a Chianti and *Goodfellas* on DVD: now that's a really good Sunday night.

To make the tomato sauce, put the olive oil, garlic, onion, tomatoes, and basil in a saucepan, season well, and bring to a boil. Reduce the heat and simmer gently for at least 40 minutes while you prepare the meatballs.

Preheat the oven to 400°F. To make the meatballs, put the beef, bread crumbs, eggs, Parmesan, parsley, and olive oil in a large mixing bowl, season, and combine with your hands. Shape the mixture into roughly 20 walnut-size balls and put in a single layer on a baking sheet covered with foil. Roast for 10 minutes, turn, then roast for a further 6–7 minutes.

Put a saucepan of salted water on to boil for the spaghetti. When it comes to a boil, drop in the spaghetti and cook according to the manufacturer's instructions until al dente. Drain, return to the pan, and add the tomato sauce and meatballs. Stir very gently so as not to break up the meatballs. Take out the onion wedges if you prefer. Transfer to bowls and sprinkle with basil and grated Parmesan.

Three-cheese risotto
with grappa and prosciutto

1 quart flavorful vegetable stock

3 tablespoons butter

1 onion, finely chopped

1½ cups risotto rice

3½ tablespoons grappa, vodka, or white wine

½ cup freshly grated Parmesan cheese

2½ oz fontina cheese, cubed

2 oz Gorgonzola Piccante, cubed

1 tablespoon extra virgin olive oil

a small handful of fresh sage leaves

4 slices prosciutto, cut into strips

freshly ground black pepper

Serves 4

This is true comfort food: indulgently cheesy with a salty edge and creamy consistency. It's reminiscent of casseroles you might have eaten as a kid, but this is strictly for adults as the grappa has a real kick!

Put the vegetable stock in a saucepan over low heat so it is gently bubbling away. Put half the butter and the onion in a heavy-based medium pan, cover, and cook over medium heat for 8 minutes, stirring occasionally until the onion is soft and translucent.

Add the rice and toss in the buttery onion for a couple of minutes. When the rice seems about to stick, pour in the grappa and a ladleful of stock. When the liquid has nearly evaporated, start adding more hot stock a ladleful at a time, lovingly stirring it until the rice absorbs it and it starts to feel like it might stick again. Continue to add stock until the rice is swollen and is no longer chalky in the center. This should take about 18–20 minutes.

Add the remaining butter and the three cheeses. Take off the heat and cover with a lid. Leave for a couple of minutes, until the butter and cheese have melted, then take off the lid and stir thoroughly.

Meanwhile, heat the oil in a skillet over high heat and quickly fry the sage leaves. Remove with a slotted spoon, then add the prosciutto to the skillet and fry for 30 seconds, or until crispy. Transfer the risotto to bowls and sprinkle with freshly ground black pepper and the crispy sage leaves and prosciutto.

Rice and Grains

To lift your stir-fries out of the ordinary and into the sublime, you need to be a bit crafty with ingredients. Both lemon grass and kaffir lime leaves can be tricky to find, but they freeze well so keep a few stored in the freezer for meals such as this.

Stir-fried tofu and vegetables
with lemon grass, lime leaves, and honey

1 tablespoon safflower oil

⅓ cup cashew nuts

2 large red chiles, sliced (and seeded if you prefer it mild)

1 lemon grass stalk (outer layer discarded), finely minced

2 kaffir lime leaves, shredded

2 garlic cloves, peeled and crushed

1 inch fresh ginger, sliced

8 oz silken tofu, cubed

8 oz medium asparagus tips

2 red bell peppers, cut into strips

1 tablespoon tamarind paste

2 tablespoons dark soy sauce

1 tablespoon honey

Serves 4

Heat the oil in a wok or a large skillet over medium/low heat and add the cashew nuts, chiles, lemon grass, lime leaves, garlic, and ginger. Gently sauté for 1 minute.

Add the tofu, asparagus, and bell peppers and stir-fry for a further 2 minutes until they start to soften around the edges and the cashew nuts turn golden.

Pour in the tamarind paste, soy sauce, and honey, along with ⅓ cup water and turn up the heat to bring the liquid to a boil. Allow the contents of the wok to bubble up so that the liquid finishes cooking the vegetables and they are lovely and tender. This should take a further 3 minutes or so.

Transfer to bowls. Remove the slices of ginger, unless you particularly like hits of feisty ginger! Serve piping hot with steamed rice or egg noodles.

Thai chicken larb

1 tablespoon white rice

2 celery ribs, thinly sliced

1 red onion, thinly sliced

1 lb cooked chicken, shredded

2 tablespoons fresh
mint leaves

¼ cup cilantro leaves

8 oz cherry tomatoes,
quartered

¼ teaspoon cayenne pepper

8 Boston lettuce leaves

sticky rice, to serve (optional)

Dressing

5 tablespoons freshly
squeezed lime juice

3 tablespoons Thai fish sauce

3 tablespoons palm sugar or
natural cane sugar

1 garlic clove, peeled
and crushed

a coffee mill

Serves 4

Larb is eaten all over Thailand and Laos. It's usually served with sticky rice and scooped up with the fingers. The trick is to get the balance right between the salty fish sauce, sour-sweet lime, and heat from the cayenne. The ground rice may seem a little unusual but it adds a good crunch and a distinctive flavor. Chopped, toasted peanuts can be substituted.

Put the rice in a skillet and toast until golden. Grind in a coffee mill until very fine.

To make the dressing, combine the lime juice, fish sauce, a touch of palm sugar, and the garlic, then taste. Add more of the sugar if you prefer it sweeter.

Mix the celery, onion, and chicken in a bowl and pour over the dressing. Just before serving, stir in the mint, cilantro, tomatoes, and cayenne pepper, to taste. Transfer to bowls lined with the lettuce leaves and serve with sticky rice, if desired.

I had these deep-fried eggs in a restaurant in Sydney and have been addicted to them ever since. I adore their frazzled whites and molten yolks. I like to tear up the egg with my chopsticks and mix it into the rice.

Deep-fried eggs
with rice, chile, and oyster sauce

¾ **cup jasmine or long-grain rice, washed**

⅔ **cup vegetable stock**

⅔ **cup peanut oil**

4 **large eggs**

2 **garlic cloves, peeled and crushed**

4 **scallions, sliced**

1 **teaspoon sesame oil**

1 **tablespoon light soy sauce**

a **good pinch of white pepper**

2 **tablespoons oyster sauce**

2 **red chiles, seeded and finely chopped**

a **handful of cilantro leaves**

Serves 2

Put the rice and stock in a small saucepan, cover, and cook over high heat. Once it is boiling, reduce the heat as low as it will go and let bubble away gently for 8–10 minutes, or until the rice has swelled and absorbed all the water. Turn off the heat and let it steam on its own for another 10 minutes.

Pour the peanut oil into a wok or large saucepan and heat until hot—throw in a cube of bread and if it browns in 10 seconds, the oil is hot enough. Crack 2 of the eggs into a dish, then gently slide them into the wok. It will hiss and splutter so stand back for a couple of seconds. Cook for 1–2 minutes until the whites are set but the yolks still oozy, then transfer with a slotted spoon onto a plate. Cook the remaining eggs in the same way.

Pour away all but 1 tablespoon of the peanut oil (you can bottle it and use it again once cool) and add the garlic. Cook until it is starting to color, then tip in the cooked rice and half the scallions. Stir-fry briskly, then add the sesame oil, soy sauce, and white pepper. Give it a good stir, then transfer to 2 bowls. Put a portion of egg on each mound of rice, drizzle with oyster sauce, and sprinkle over the chiles, remaining scallions, and the cilantro leaves.

Couscous with feta, dill, and spring beans

1¾ cups couscous

1¾ cups boiling water

5 tablespoons extra virgin olive oil

1 garlic clove, peeled and crushed

3 shallots, peeled and thinly sliced

2 tablespoons chopped fresh dill

2 tablespoons snipped fresh chives

1 tablespoon finely chopped preserved lemon, or 1 tablespoon peel and flesh of fresh lemon, finely chopped

8 oz feta cheese, chopped

5 oz sugar snap peas

5 oz baby fava beans

5 oz frozen peas, defrosted

freshly ground black pepper

Serves 4

Dill is a herb that has never been terribly fashionable, unlike its peers, rosemary and sage. It's quite a floral, grassy herb and a whiff of it conjures up springtime, which is possibly why it is so well complemented by the beans and peas in this dish. Marinating the feta lifts it from a salty, creamy cheese to something much more complex, so it's well worth it, even if it's just for 5 minutes.

Put the couscous in a large bowl and pour over the boiling water. Cover with plastic wrap or a plate and let swell for 10 minutes.

Pour the olive oil into a mixing bowl and add the garlic, shallots, dill, chives, and preserved lemon and lots of freshly ground black pepper—the coarser the better. Add the feta, turn in the oil, and set aside while you cook the beans.

Bring a medium saucepan of unsalted water to a boil. Add the sugar snap peas, bring back to a boil, and cook for 1 minute. Add the fava beans, bring back to a boil, and cook for 1 minute. Finally, add the peas and cook for 2 minutes. Drain.

Uncover the couscous, stir in the hot beans, transfer to bowls, and top with the feta, spooning over the flavored oil as you go. Stir well before serving.

Cumin-spiced lamb chops
with chickpea mash and roasted vine tomatoes

8 large or 12 medium lamb chops, trimmed of fat

2 tablespoons extra virgin olive oil, plus extra to drizzle

1 teaspoon cumin seeds

two 14-oz cans chickpeas, drained

10 oz vine cherry tomatoes

¼ cup chopped cilantro

sea salt and freshly ground black pepper

Marinade

2 tablespoons extra virgin olive oil

2 tablespoons chopped fresh mint

finely grated peel of 1 unwaxed lemon, plus 5 tablespoons juice

1 teaspoon ground red pepper

1 garlic clove, peeled and crushed

Serves 4

The lemony, minty marinade is perfect here with lamb chops that are broiled to rosy perfection. It's also very good with chicken, shrimp, and fish. The chickpea mash is made very easy by using canned chickpeas and you'll find that mashing by hand produces a less gluey result than using a food processor.

To make the marinade, combine the olive oil, mint, lemon peel and 1 tablespoon of the juice, the ground red pepper, and garlic in a large bowl. Add the lamb chops, season well, and toss. If you have time, marinate for an hour; if not, move swiftly on.

Heat ½ tablespoon of the olive oil in a skillet over medium heat, add the cumin seeds and stir for 30 seconds until fragrant. Tip in the chickpeas and toss in the oil for 1 minute. Stir in the remaining lemon juice and ⅓ cup water, cover, and simmer for 10 minutes until softened. Preheat the broiler to high.

Put the lamb chops on a baking sheet lined with aluminum foil and broil for 5–6 minutes until blackened around the edges. Turn over, add the tomatoes (halving any large ones), drizzle with the remaining olive oil, season, and broil for a further 5–6 minutes.

Mash the chickpeas with a potato masher until you get a chunky purée. Add the cilantro, season to taste, and stir. Transfer to bowls and top with 2 or 3 lamb chops. Drizzle with olive oil and lamb juices.

Lamb and fava bean tagine
with buttered couscous

2¾ lb boneless shoulder of
lamb or shoulder chops, cut
into large chunks

2 teaspoons ground cinnamon

2 teaspoons ground cumin

½ teaspoon hot ground
red pepper

1 teaspoon ground turmeric

a pinch of saffron threads

½ teaspoon ground
white pepper

2 tablespoons olive oil

3 onions, chopped

3 garlic cloves, peeled
and crushed

2½ cups hot lamb stock

1 cup dates, pitted

1 cup fava beans, shelled

cilantro, to garnish

Buttered couscous

1⅓ cups couscous

1⅓ cups boiling lamb stock

3 tablespoons butter, diced

a tagine or large casserole dish

Serves 4

Shoulder of lamb suits this sweet, spicy tagine perfectly, because it is one of the sweeter cuts of meat. Like all stews made with aromatic spices, it tastes even better the next day, once the flavors have mingled, so my advice is to pop it on the stove the night before and simply warm it up when you come home the following evening.

Put the lamb in a large bowl and toss with the cinnamon, cumin, ground red pepper, turmeric, saffron, and white pepper. Heat the olive oil in a tagine or casserole dish over high heat, then add half the lamb. Cook for a few minutes, stirring occasionally, until the lamb is evenly brown. Tip into a bowl, add more oil to the tagine dish, and brown the remainder of the lamb. Put all the lamb back in with the onions, garlic, stock, and a large pinch of salt. Bring the mixture to a boil, cover with a lid, and reduce the heat. Simmer gently for 1 hour.

Add the dates to the tagine and simmer for a further 20 minutes.

Add the fava beans and simmer for a further 10 minutes. The tagine should have been cooking for 1½ hours and the meat should be so tender that it falls apart easily.

When the tagine is ready, put the couscous in a large bowl, pour over the stock, and add the butter. Cover with plastic wrap or a plate and let swell for 6–7 minutes.

Fluff up the couscous with a fork and serve with the tagine. Garnish with cilantro.

Pan-fried steaks
with new potatoes, Roquefort, and arugula

1½ lb new potatoes

four 8-oz sirloin or rib-eye
steaks (1 inch thick)

5 tablespoons good-quality
extra virgin olive oil

1 garlic clove, peeled
and crushed

2 tablespoons capers

finely grated peel and juice of
1 unwaxed lemon

2 oz arugula

2½ oz Roquefort cheese

sea salt and freshly ground
black pepper

a heavy griddle

Serves 4

Cooking steaks well is all about getting the pan very hot and creating a golden crust on the meat which prevents any juices from escaping. Let them rest after cooking and squeeze over lemon juice (an Italian trick), which cuts through the richness of the meat. When finishing the potatoes, don't be stingy with the olive oil: use a liberal amount of good-quality, grassy, fruity oil because it's not being cooked so you really taste the flavors.

Put a medium saucepan of water on to boil. Add a large pinch of salt and the potatoes. Simmer gently for 20–22 minutes until very tender, then drain and return to the pan.

Meanwhile, heat a heavy griddle or large skillet over very high heat. Drizzle the steaks with 1 tablespoon of the olive oil and season. When the pan is smoking, add the steaks. Let them cook, without turning them over, for 3 minutes. Now turn them over and cook for a further 2–3 minutes. Prod them to check if they are done to your liking: a little give means medium and lots of give means rare. Transfer them to a plate, tent with aluminum foil, and let rest for a few minutes.

Mix the remaining olive oil with the garlic, capers, and lemon peel in a small pitcher, season well, and set aside. Lightly crush the potatoes with the back of a spoon until they buckle a little, then fold in the arugula and olive oil. Crumble over the Roquefort cheese and transfer to bowls. Pour the lemon juice all over the steaks and cut into strips. Lift onto the potatoes, pour over any steak juices, and sprinkle with freshly ground black pepper.

Herby sausages with polenta
and rosemary, red onion, and red currant gravy

8 herb-flavor sausages

sea salt and freshly ground black pepper

Rosemary, red onion, and red currant gravy

2 tablespoons olive oil

2 red onions, thinly sliced

2 rosemary sprigs, broken up

2 teaspoons flour

2 tablespoons red currant jelly

1¼ cups red wine

1¼ cups beef stock

2 tablespoons butter

Polenta

1 cup fine cornmeal

3½ tablespoons butter

¾ cup freshly grated Parmesan cheese

Serves 4

This is my Italian take on sausage and mash with a bit of British red currant jelly thrown in because I love the way it makes onion gravy sticky. If you've tried polenta (cornmeal) before and weren't blown away, try it again now: the secret, as with most of the good things in life, is lots of butter, cheese, and seasoning.

Put 3 cups water in a medium pan over high heat, cover, and heat until it simmers.

Pour the cornmeal into the pan of simmering water and beat out any lumps. Reduce the heat to low and bubble away for 30 minutes or according to the manufacturer's instructions.

To make the rosemary, red onion, and red currant gravy, heat the olive oil in a skillet and start cooking the onions and rosemary over medium heat, stirring. When the onions are beginning to soften, reduce the heat, cover, and let soften slowly in their own juices. After 10–15 minutes, stir in the flour and cook for about 1 minute until it is no longer pale. Add the jelly, wine, and stock and bring to a boil. Let bubble away gently for 15 minutes while you cook the sausages.

Preheat the broiler. Put the sausages on a baking sheet lined with aluminum foil and broil for 15 minutes, turning halfway through.

When everything is ready, beat the butter and Parmesan into the polenta and season. Beat the butter into the gravy and season to taste. Transfer the polenta to bowls, top with 2 sausages, and pour over the hot gravy.

Chicken and lentil curry
with cucumber yogurt

2 tablespoons butter or ghee

2 large onions, thinly sliced

2 garlic cloves, peeled
and crushed

1½ tablespoons garam masala
(or ¼ teaspoon grated nutmeg;
½ teaspoon ground cinnamon;
½ teaspoon ground pepper;
1 teaspoon ground cumin; and
10 cardamom pods, crushed)

1 lb boneless chicken thigh or
breast meat, cut into chunks

1¼ cups tomato juice

8 bay or curry leaves

⅔ cup red lentils

1¾ cups chicken stock

sea salt and freshly ground
black pepper

cilantro leaves, to serve
(optional)

mango chutney and warm
chapattis, to serve (optional)

Cucumber yogurt

⅔ cup plain yogurt

¼ cucumber, cut into ribbons
or chopped

Serves 4

The authentic flavor of a curry comes from using fresh spices (not ones that have been lurking in your very own kitchen graveyard) and the heady, slightly sour taste of bay leaves. Chicken thighs work better here than breast meat as they are harder to overcook.

Melt the butter in a deep skillet, add the onions, and fry, stirring, over medium heat. Once they are sizzling, cover with a lid, reduce the heat, and cook for 10–15 minutes, stirring occasionally.

When the onions have softened, add the garlic and garam masala, cook for a further 3–4 minutes until the spices start to release their aroma and the onions are beginning to turn golden. If you are using chicken thighs, add them now and cook for 5–6 minutes. Add the tomato juice, bay leaves, lentils, and stock. If you are using chicken breast, add it now. Cover with a lid and simmer for 15 minutes until the lentils are tender.

To make the cucumber yogurt, put the yogurt in a small dish, add a good pinch of salt, and stir in the cucumber.

When the curry is cooked, season generously with salt and freshly ground black pepper (lentils tend to absorb a lot of seasoning so don't be stingy). Transfer to bowls, scatter with cilantro, if using, and serve with a dollop of the cucumber yogurt to mix in. Serve with mango chutney and warm chapattis, rolled up, if desired.

Shiitake mushrooms have a unique, earthy savoriness that few other non-meaty ingredients have and which the Japanese call *umami*. This means they can make a light broth very flavorful. Soba noodles are made from buckwheat and go well with the delicate salmon.

Salmon, soba noodle,
and shiitake broth

1 tablespoon peanut oil

8 oz shiitake mushrooms, washed, dried and halved

1¼ inches fresh ginger, sliced

three ¼-oz sachets miso stock powder

3 quarts boiling water

6½ oz buckwheat soba noodles

2 tablespoons light soy sauce

¼ cup sake (rice wine)

2 tablespoons granulated sugar

four 4-oz salmon fillets, cut into chunks

6 scallions, sliced

a pinch of ground red pepper

sesame oil, to drizzle

Serves 4

Heat the oil in a large saucepan over medium heat and add the mushrooms and ginger. Cook gently for 5 minutes, or until softened.

Put the miso stock powder and boiling water in a pitcher and stir until dissolved. Pour into the pan with the mushrooms. Bring to a boil and simmer for 5 minutes to allow the flavors to infuse. Add the noodles and bring to a boil, then cook for a further 4 minutes, or until just tender (they will continue to cook while you dish up so don't overdo them). Add the soy sauce, sake, and sugar to the broth and gently lower in the salmon. Reduce the heat to low so the broth is only just boiling and poach the salmon for 3–4 minutes, or until cooked through.

Fish out the noodles and transfer to bowls. Using a slotted spoon, lift out the salmon and place on top of the noodles. Ladle the remaining soup into the bowls, scatter with the scallions and ground red pepper, and drizzle with sesame oil.

Thai curry is a great flavor hit when you get in from a busy day. Ready-made pastes make everything easier but your curry will only be as good as your paste. Look for Thai brands, which are good but can often be very hot, or make your own and freeze it in small portions.

Red curry with shrimp and pumpkin

a 14-oz can coconut milk

2 tablespoons red curry paste

2 tablespoons palm sugar
or natural cane sugar

1 lemon grass stalk, cut in half
and bruised

14 oz pie pumpkin or butternut
squash, peeled, seeded, and
cut into 1-inch chunks

4 oz sugar snap peas,
cut diagonally

6½ oz uncooked tiger shrimp,
shelled, deveined, and
butterflied but tails intact

2 tablespoons Thai fish sauce

15 fresh mint leaves,
finely shredded

1 large red chile, seeded and
cut into thin strips

steamed jasmine rice, to serve

Serves 4

If you remember, put the coconut milk in the refrigerator as soon as you buy it.

When you are ready to start cooking, scrape off the thick coconut cream that usually clings to the lid and put just the cream in a wok or large saucepan over medium heat. Add the curry paste and stir for 1–2 minutes until the paste smells fragrant, then add the sugar and cook for a further 2 minutes until sticky.

Pour in the rest of the coconut milk, add the lemon grass, pumpkin, and ⅓–½ cup water to almost cover the pumpkin. Bring the contents of the wok to a gentle simmer and let bubble away gently for 10 minutes, or until the pumpkin is tender.

Add the sugar snap peas and cook for 2 minutes, then add the shrimp and cook for a further 2 minutes or until they turn pink. Remove from the heat and stir in the fish sauce. Transfer to bowls and sprinkle with the mint and chile. Taste and add more fish sauce if necessary. Serve with steamed jasmine rice.

Figs roasted in Madeira
with pine nuts and fudgy Greek yogurt

8 fresh figs

⅛ cup Madeira

3 tablespoons pine nuts

⅛ cup dark muscovado or packed brown sugar

6½ oz thick Greek yogurt

a baking dish

Serves 4

Figs roasted in the oven with a splash of warming alcohol positively ooze succulence and sweetness. The voluptuous Greek yogurt is so stiff you could stand a spoon in it, and it becomes gorgeously fudgy when scattered with rich muscovado sugar.

Preheat the oven to 400°F.

Cut the stalks off the figs and cut a cross in the top about one-third of the way through. Stand them in a baking dish, pour over the Madeira, and scatter with the nuts and half the sugar. Bake for 20–25 minutes, basting occasionally.

Spoon the yogurt into 4 bowls and scatter with the remaining sugar. Let stand for 10 minutes until it absorbs the sugar and turns slightly fudgy in texture.

When the figs are cooked and on the verge of collapsing gracefully, transfer them to the bowls next to the fudgy yogurt and pour over the hot sticky juices.

Desserts

Pine nuts and almonds with their toasty flavors add another dimension to this crumble. Slightly sour, juicy plums, in my mind, were made for crumbles. The soft brown sugar thickens the plum juices to create a burgundy caramel that bubbles up to stain the nutty crust. The crust is quite biscuity so it will need to settle before it crisps up, which is perfect because crumbles are best eaten warm rather than piping hot.

Nutty plum crumble

12 plums, halved and pitted

2–3 thick strips of peel and the juice from 1 unwaxed orange

⅓ cup packed brown sugar

1 stick unsalted butter, chilled and diced

¾ cup self-rising flour

⅓ cup ground almonds

3 tablespoons slivered almonds

3 tablespoons pine nuts

fresh cream, to serve

a baking dish

Serves 4

Preheat the oven to 350°F.

Put the plums in the baking dish—there should be enough room left to accommodate the crumble topping. Add the orange peel and juice. Sprinkle over 2 tablespoons of the sugar and dot over 2 tablespoons of the butter. Cover with aluminum foil and bake for 25–30 minutes, or until the plums are beginning to soften.

Put the flour, ground almonds, and the remaining butter in a bowl (or a food processor) and rub (or pulse) until it forms lumps. Rub in the slivered almonds, pine nuts, and the remaining sugar.

Remove the baking dish from the oven, discard the foil, and scatter over the crumble topping. Bake for 30 minutes, or until the topping is golden and the juices are bubbling through. Remove from the oven and let stand for 10 minutes to allow the crust to firm up. Transfer to bowls and serve with cream.

This is such a simple but delicious dessert that you feel it must be bad for you. In fact, fresh fruit and fragrant honey are all that are needed to make this so good, so why not treat yourself to a large scoop of vanilla ice cream on the side!

Peaches poached in
vanilla honey syrup

2 tablespoons orange-blossom honey

1 vanilla bean, sliced lengthwise

4 peaches, unpeeled, pitted, and halved

4 oz fresh raspberries

vanilla ice cream, to serve (optional)

Serves 4

Place 1 cup water, the honey, and vanilla bean in a large saucepan. Bring to a boil over high heat, then reduce the heat, cover, and simmer gently for 5 minutes to allow the vanilla to impart its flavor.

Add the peaches and return to a boil. Continue to simmer for 3–4 minutes until the peaches are soft. Remove the peaches from the pan with a slotted spoon.

While the peaches cool for a few minutes, boil the remaining syrup in the pan until it reduces by about half.

When the peaches are cool enough to handle, peel off their skins, which should come off like little jackets. Serve a couple of peach halves in a bowl with some raspberries and drizzle with the syrup. Serve with a large scoop of ice cream, if desired.

Chocolate brownies
with vanilla-flecked crème fraîche

8 oz semisweet chocolate, broken into pieces

2 sticks unsalted butter, softened

4 large eggs, beaten

1¾ cups sugar

½ teaspoon salt

1 cup self-rising flour

2 tablespoons unsweetened cocoa

¾ cup crème fraîche or very lightly whipped heavy cream

1 vanilla bean, cut lengthwise and seeds scraped out

a baking pan, 8 x 12 inches, greased and lined with parchment paper

Makes 16 brownies

It's easy to think your brownies aren't cooked and to give them those extra few minutes, which can dry them out and turn them into a mealy chocolate cake. So be brave: if the mixture doesn't wobble in the middle and a skewer inserted in the center comes out chocolatey, remove the brownies from the oven and by the time they have cooled, they will be perfect. I love the sour edge crème fraîche has over the sweetness of the chocolate.

Preheat the oven to 350°F. Don't use a convection oven if you have the choice, as it dries the outside of the brownies.

Put the chocolate and butter in a heatproof bowl set over a pan of simmering water and leave for several minutes until melted, then remove from the pan and let cool.

Beat together the eggs and the sugar with an electric mixer. Pour in the cooled chocolate mixture, then add the salt and finally the flour. Beat until well blended. Pour the mixture into the prepared baking pan and bake in the center of the oven for 23–25 minutes (you have to be precise with brownies!). The outside should look crackled and the inside will feel firm to the touch but will be gooey underneath. Remove from the oven and let cool in the pan for 15 minutes, then slice into squares.

Mix the crème fraîche with the vanilla seeds and serve with a brownie square or two.

It takes a while to get the hang of properly peeling oranges so they are pith-free but it's worth the effort. The fruit you end up with is refreshing and sharp, which is why it contrasts so well with the sticky, sweet caramel. The preserved ginger warms up the dish and complements the orange beautifully.

Ginger and caramel oranges

¾ **cup sugar**

1¼ inches fresh ginger, peeled and sliced

½ cup heavy cream

1 tablespoon butter

5 navel oranges

2 balls of ginger from a jar of stem ginger preserved in syrup, drained and diced

Serves 4

Put the sugar, ⅓ cup water, and the fresh ginger in a medium pan over low heat and heat gently until the sugar has dissolved. Turn up the heat and boil until the edges start to turn golden. Without stirring the syrup, swirl the pan until the syrup is an even teak color. Pour in another ⅓ cup water and the heavy cream to thin the syrup down to a runny caramel. Add the butter and set aside to cool slightly.

Cut the tops and bases off the oranges so they stand flat on a cutting board. Using a small, serrated knife, cut off the skin and pith, following the curve of the orange, all the way round until you have taken off all the pith. Slice the remaining orange flesh thinly.

Transfer the oranges to bowls, scatter with the preserved ginger, and drizzle with the caramel. Serve by itself, with vanilla ice cream, or with a spice-infused ice cream, such as cardamom.

index

conversion chart

Weights and measures have been rounded up or down slightly to make measuring easier.

Measuring butter:
A US stick of butter weighs 4 oz which is approximately 115 g or 8 tablespoons. The recipes in this book require the following conversions:

American	Metric	Imperial
6 tbsp	85 g	3 oz
7 tbsp	100 g	3½ oz
1 stick	115 g	4 oz

Volume equivalents:

American	Metric	Imperial
1 teaspoon	5 ml	
1 tablespoon	15 ml	
¼ cup	60 ml	2 fl oz
⅓ cup	75 ml	2½ fl oz
½ cup	125 ml	4 fl oz
⅔ cup	150 ml	5 fl oz (¼ pint)
¾ cup	175 ml	6 fl oz
1 cup	250 ml	8 fl oz

Weight equivalents:

Imperial	Metric
1 oz	30 g
2 oz	55 g
3 oz	85 g
3½ oz	100 g
4 oz	115 g
6 oz	175 g
8 oz (½ lb)	225 g
9 oz	250 g
10 oz	280 g
12 oz	350 g
13 oz	375 g
14 oz	400 g
15 oz	425 g
16 oz (1 lb)	450 g

Measurements:

Inches	cm
¼ inch	5 mm
½ inch	1 cm
1 inch	2.5 cm
2 inches	5 cm
3 inches	7 cm
4 inches	10 cm
5 inches	12 cm
6 inches	15 cm
7 inches	18 cm
8 inches	20 cm
9 inches	23 cm
10 inches	25 cm
11 inches	28 cm
12 inches	30 cm

Oven temperatures:

120°C	(250°F)	Gas ½
140°C	(275°F)	Gas 1
150°C	(300°F)	Gas 2
170°C	(325°F)	Gas 3
180°C	(350°F)	Gas 4
190°C	(375°F)	Gas 5
200°C	(400°F)	Gas 6